The Sabotage

How the USA Planned to Undermine
China's Belt and Road Project

GEW Reports & Analyses Team

Global East-West for Research & Studies

Contents

Chapter 1

Introduction to "The Sabotage"

The quest for dominance and influence has emerged as a defining characteristic of our modern world in an era of constantly intensifying competition on a global scale. At the core of this intricate and multifaceted rivalry lies the audacious Belt and Road Initiative (BRI), championed by China—a monumental shift in global economics and geopolitics. "The Sabotage" delves profoundly into the intricacies of this worldwide power struggle, unveiling the meticulously orchestrated strategic responses enacted by the United States to counter and challenge the continually expanding reach of China's BRI.

The BRI, conceived by Chinese President Xi Jinping,

envisions bolstering connectivity, trade, and infrastructure development across vast expanses of Asia, Europe, Africa, and beyond, fostering economic integration and regional cooperation. However, this audacious endeavour has not merely reshaped the global trade and governance framework. It has also ignited substantial resentment among Western powers, most notably the United States. Perceiving the burgeoning influence of China as a potential threat to its global supremacy, the United States has adopted a multifaceted approach in a last effort to stop, contain, or hinder the ambitions of the BRI.

The present work presents a first analysis of the United States' strategic manoeuvres, focusing on creating the India-Middle East-Europe Corridor (IMEEC)—an alternative trade route designed to circumvent China's dominance. By cultivating strategic alliances with key nations in the Middle East and Europe, the United States endeavours to re-establish its shaky position in the global hierarchy and present a counterbalance to China's ascending and, according to many international observers, unstoppable pre-eminence.

"The Sabotage" not only delves into the geopolitical duel between these two – ascending Vs descending – global powers, but also scrutinises the broader ramifications of these actions on regional and international politics. From deploying intricate diplomatic and economic strategies to fortifying alliances and providing unwavering security assurances, the United States employs a gamut of tactics to adeptly navigate the intricate dynamics of the region and address pressing local concerns. The strategic recontrol and realignment of pivotal nations such as Saudi Arabia and the United Arab Emirates, becoming too much independent in the American eyes, further underscores the ever-evolving geopolitical landscape.

As we delve into the intricacies of this global power struggle, "The Sabotage" unfurls a riveting narrative that underscores the desperate attempt of the United States, as it is losing speed, to uphold a delicate balance of power and safeguard its strategic interests in the face of China's ever-expanding influence. Through collaborative partnerships, ambitious infrastructure development initiatives, and a delusory commitment to regional security and stability, the United States intend to assert its role in shaping the emerging world order to its own image (what a waste of time!), navigating the challenges of China's Belt and Road Initiative.

Chapter 2

The Battle for Global Influence: US IMEEC Vs China BRI

A s the world enters a new era of geopolitical competition, the battle for global influence has become a defining feature of our time. Countries are vying to assert their power, secure their interests, and shape the international order to their advantage. At the forefront of this struggle are two dominant forces: the emerging superpower, China, and the reigning global power, the United States.

The rise of China as an economic powerhouse and its

growing global influence have challenged the long-standing dominance of the United States. China's ambitious Belt and Road Initiative (BRI) has become a symbol of its aspirations for greater connectivity, economic expansion, and diplomatic clout. Through a network of infrastructure projects across Asia, Africa, and Europe, China aims to expand its influence, secure vital resources, and create new trade routes.

The BRI has sparked concerns among Western powers, especially the United States, as it sees China's growing influence as a threat to its own global dominance. The United States has responded by adopting a multi-faceted approach aimed at countering China's expansionist agenda. One strategy is the development of *the India-Middle East-Europe Corridor (IMEEC)*, which seeks to create an alternative trade route that bypasses China's dominance.

The IMEEC project is part of a broader effort by the United States to obstruct China's BRI. It aims to strengthen ties with India, a rising power in Asia, and leverage its strategic location as a gateway between the Middle East and Europe. This corridor offers an alternative route for goods and energy supplies, reducing dependence on China and undermining its economic leverage.

To execute this strategy effectively, the United States has

been working tirelessly to forge transnational rail and port agreements along the IMEEC route. These agreements establish a framework for cooperation among countries involved, ensuring seamless connectivity and enhancing trade relations. By facilitating the movement of goods and resources, the United States aims to establish itself as a key player and diminish China's influence.

However, obstructing China's BRI is no easy task. China has been successful in cultivating relationships with countries through infrastructure investments, economic aid, and trade partnerships. Winning over these countries and convincing them to turn away from China requires strategic manoeuvring and attractive incentives. The United States must navigate complex regional dynamics, address local concerns, and present itself as a viable alternative to China.

Moreover, a significant challenge in this battle for global influence lies in the discord within the BRICS alliance (Brazil, Russia, India, China, and South Africa + from January 2024, Argentina, Egypt, Ethiopia, Iran, Saudi Arabia and UAE). The United States aims to exploit divisions within the alliance, particularly focusing on India, to weaken China's support base. By bolstering ties with India and offering it an influential role in shaping the new world order, the United States hopes to fracture the unity among the BRICS and reduce China's collective influence.

The Gulf Arab countries, an important region for both China and the United States, are also witnessing a strategic shift. Traditionally aligned with the United States, countries like Saudi Arabia and the United Arab Emirates (UAE) are now seeking to diversify their alliances and reduce dependence on any one power. The IMEEC project opens up avenues for the United States to regain control over these influential countries, thus undermining China's presence in the region.

To effectively obstruct China's projects in the Middle East, the United States will employ a combination of diplomatic, economic, and strategic manoeuvres. Strengthening alliances, providing security assurances, and presenting attractive economic opportunities are essential components of this strategy. The United States will also have to leverage existing tensions and rivalries in the region to its advantage.

The battle for global influence between China and the United States is complex and multifaceted. While China's Belt and Road Initiative poses a challenge to the United States' global dominance, the United States is not backing down. Through initiatives such as the IMEEC and strategic engagement with key partners, the United States aims to counter China's growing influence and maintain its own position at the centre of the global stage.

References and Further Reading:

1. Institute for Security Studies. (2021). Belt and Road Initiative: Understanding challenges and implications.

2. Council on Foreign Relations. (2021). China's Belt and Road Initiative: Five Years Later.

3. Rand Corporation. (2021). Assessing the Impact of China's Belt and Road Initiative.

4. European Parliament. (2021). EU collective strategic thinking on China: Balancing engagement and specific interests.

5. Center for Strategic and International Studies. (2021). Courtship and coercion: The dual strategy of Chinese investment.

6. Chatham House. (2021). The Belt and Road Initiative: Implications for the global economy.

7. Brookings Institution. (2021). Competing visions for connectivity: China's Belt and Road Initiative vs. the United States' Free and Open Indo-Pacific.

8. The White House. (2021). Build Back Better World Partnership: Advancing infrastructure investment.

9. U.S. Department of State. (2021). United States-India Collaboration on Smart Cities Development.

10. Nikkei Asia. (2021). US builds India-Europe trade route to rival China's Belt and Road.

11. The World Bank. (2021). Belt and Road Initiative: Providing opportunities or creating risks?

12. U.S. Chamber of Commerce. (2021). India's role in the Indo-Pacific strategy.

13. Peterson Institute for International Economics. (2021). China's Belt and Road Initiative: an introduction.

14. Asia Society. (2021). The Belt and Road Initiative – a new phase in China's economic diplomacy.

Chapter 3

The Rise of China's Belt and Road Initiative

The Rise of China's Belt and Road Initiative signifies a monumental shift in global economic and geopolitical dynamics. The goal of this ambitious project, which Chinese President Xi Jinping proposed in 2013, is to improve infrastructure development, trade, and connectivity across Asia, Europe, Africa, and beyond. The Belt and Road Initiative (BRI) encompasses a vast network of roads, railways, ports, and other infrastructure projects, fostering economic integration and regional cooperation. This chapter delves into the origins, objectives, and implications of China's Belt and Road Initiative, analysing its impact on global trade, governance, and the existing international order.

Origins and Objectives:

China's Belt and Road Initiative draws inspiration from the ancient Silk Road, which connected civilisations and facilitated extensive trade in goods, knowledge, and culture. Under the BRI, China aims to reestablish economic links and strengthen cooperation between countries along the historical Silk Road, while also expanding connectivity and partnerships across new regions. The multifaceted objectives of the BRI include promoting economic development, facilitating trade, enhancing financial connectivity, and fostering people-to-people exchanges. Furthermore, China seeks to solidify its position as a global economic leader, achieve sustainable growth, and address domestic challenges through external engagements.

Geographical Scope and Key Projects:

The Belt and Road Initiative spans across multiple continents and encompasses various land and maritime routes. The "Belt" refers to the overland

Silk Road Economic Belt, which includes six corridors: the New Eurasian Land Bridge Economic Corridor, the China-Mongolia-Russia Economic Corridor, the China-Central Asia-West Asia Economic Corridor, the China-Indochina Peninsula Economic Corridor, the China-Pakistan Economic Corridor, and the Bangladesh-China-India-Myanmar Economic Corridor. The "Road" refers to the 21st Century Maritime Silk Road, connecting China with Southeast Asia, South Asia, the Middle East, Africa, and Europe.

Key infrastructure projects under the BRI include the construction of railways, highways, pipelines, ports, industrial parks, and telecommunications networks. The China-Pakistan Economic Corridor (CPEC), for instance, is a flagship project that involves the development of a network of energy projects, highways, and special economic zones in Pakistan, connecting China's western regions with the Arabian Sea. Similarly, the China-Mongolia-Russia Economic Corridor aims to enhance trade and connectivity between the three countries, focusing on infrastructure development, energy cooperation, and agricultural cooperation.

Implications and Criticism:

The Belt and Road Initiative has significant implications for global economic and geopolitical dynamics. Advocates argue that it fosters economic development, promotes regional integration, and creates win-win opportunities for participating countries. They highlight the potential for job creation, improved infrastructure, enhanced connectivity, and increased trade and investment. Chinese authorities have also stressed the compatibility of the BRI with existing regional and global frameworks aiming to bolster cooperation and development.

However, critics raise concerns regarding China's strategic motives, debt sustainability of participating countries, environmental impact, lack of transparency, and potential for geopolitical rivalries. They argue that the BRI allows China to extend its influence and reshape the existing international order, challenging the dominance of established powers such as the United States. They don't say why the world should accept the same dominant powers forever, as this is exactly what they wish and imply in their argument. Additionally, they pretend to have concerns about the impact of Chinese-financed projects on indigenous communities and potential for exploitative labour practices, which is an odd objection coming from the defenders of a capitalist system whose victims are millions – if not billions – of impoverished people worldwide.

Critics also worry about the financial risks associated with BRI projects. The Centre for Global Development, in a 2018 report, identified eight countries - Djibouti, Kyrgyzstan, Laos, the Maldives, Mongolia, Montenegro, Pakistan, and Tajikistan - at particular risk of debt distress due to their involvement in China's infrastructure projects. These countries face high debt burdens that may hinder their economic development and lead to undue influence from Chinese lenders. But how many countries are extremely indebted to the IMF? How many countries revolted against the IMF system? Did we forget the "Bread Revolts" in the 1980's? Even the Arab Spring revolts did not burst out because we live in a socialist international system, but well because the Arab peoples are exhausted by the same capitalism that killed millions of labourers in the mines since the 19th century.

The geopolitical implications of the BRI are significant. China's rising influence and economic power, coupled with its infrastructure development projects, have prompted other countries to either align or counter China's growing clout. India, for example, has expressed reservations about the China-Pakistan Economic Corridor, which passes through Pakistan-administered Kashmir—a region India claims as its own. Other countries, including Japan and the United States, have responded by launching their own infrastructure initiatives aimed at providing alternatives to the BRI. But none worked so far.

The United States, in particular, has raised concerns about China's expanding influence and has sought to counterbalance it by implementing a strategic response known as the Free and Open Indo-Pacific (FOIP) strategy. The FOIP strategy aims to promote a free and open regional order by enhancing connectivity, "transparent" investment, and "respect for international law" (like what we witnessed since the beginning of the Israeli genocide in Gaza in October 2023). It seeks to strengthen alliances and partnerships with countries in the Indo-Pacific region, ensuring a rules-based system that upholds "democratic values" and safeguards against undue influence.

Conclusion:

The Belt and Road Initiative represents China's ambitious endeavour to reshape global trade and exert influence over a vast network of countries through extensive infrastructure development. It has the potential to reshape regional dynamics, impact global governance, and redefine economic relationships. As the BRI continues to evolve and expand, careful analysis and evaluation, guided by academic papers, policy reports, and major press releases, are crucial to understanding its implications, both for China and the wider international community. The subsequent chapters will delve into the countermeasures and reactions of other countries, particularly the response of the United States and its strategic moves in the India-Middle East-Europe Corridor, as the battle for global influence intensifies.

References and Further Reading:

1. Duggan, Ciaran. "China's Belt and Road Initiative: Motives, Scope, and Challenges." Congressional Research Service, 2019.

2. "Belt and Road Initiative." China Development Bank Research Center, 2019.

3. Chow, Edward T. "The Belt and Road Initiative in Southeast Asia." Asia Policy, Vol. 17, No. 4, October 2020.

4. Mohan, Rovshan. "Unpacking Chinese Economic Statecraft: The Belt and Road Initiative in South Asia and Its Limits." Asia Policy, Vol. 15, No. 1, January 2020.

5. Hasselback, Drew. "The New Silk Roads: China, the US, and the Future of Globalization." Foreign Affairs, Jan/Feb 2018.

6. Burrows, Mathew. "The Belt and Road Initiative: Will Economic Synergy Overpower Geopolitics?" Harvard Kennedy School Ash Center for Democratic Governance and Innovation, 2020.

7. The World Bank Group. "Belt and Road Economics: Opportunities and Risks of Transport Corridors." World Bank, 2019.

8. McGregor, Richard. "China's Belt and Road Initiative: How Should the U.S. Respond?" Council on Foreign Relations, 2018.

9. The BRI database of the Center for Strategic and International Studies (CSIS).

Chapter 4

The USA's Countermove - The India-Middle East-Europe Corridor

As China's Belt and Road Initiative (BRI) gains momentum, the United States recognises the need to respond strategically. In this chapter, we focus on the development of the India-Middle East-Europe Corridor. By leveraging its relationships with key countries in the Middle East and Europe, the USA aims to reclaim its lost position in the global order and counterbalance China's growing dominance.

1. The Geopolitical Significance of the India-Middle East-Europe Corridor:

The Rise of India: India's emergence as a major player in the Indo-Pacific region has heightened its importance in the USA's countermove against China. With its rapidly growing economy, demographic advantage, and increasing regional influence, India presents an opportunity for the USA to strengthen its strategic partnership and counterbalance China's dominance.

The Middle East's Strategic Importance: The Middle East holds a critical position in global affairs due to its vast energy reserves, key maritime trade routes, and geopolitical significance. By "deepening" ties with (should we rather say : by tying up?) countries in the Middle East, the USA gains access to vital energy resources, enhances its ability to influence regional dynamics, and strategically counters China's presence in the region.

Europe's Role in the Countermove: Europe's geographical proximity to both Asia and the Middle East, along with its historical ties to these regions, makes it a crucial player in the India-Middle East-Europe Corridor. Europe's involvement is essential for the USA to achieve its strategic objectives of maintaining a balance of power, fostering economic ties, and countering China's increasing influence.

2. USA's Strategy in the India-Middle East-Europe Corridor:

Strengthening Partnerships:

India-USA Strategic Partnership: The USA recognises the importance of deepening its relationship with India and regards it as a key player in the Indo-Pacific region. By enhancing defence cooperation, facilitating trade and investment, and promoting shared values, the USA aims to strengthen its strategic partnership with India to counterbalance China's influence.

Middle East Allies: The USA has long-standing partnerships with key countries in the Middle East, including Saudi Arabia, United Arab Emirates (UAE), and Israel. These alliances allow the USA to maintain a military presence, ensure the security of vital energy resources, and counterbalance China's growing presence in the region. Not so an easy task, when the so-called allies have strategic agreements with China.

Transatlantic Cooperation: Recognising the importance of collaboration with European nations, especially those with key ports and trading hubs, the USA seeks to strengthen transatlantic cooperation in the India-Middle East-Europe Corridor. This cooperation includes infrastructure development, trade agreements, and security partnerships to ensure a joint approach in countering China's influence.

Infrastructure Development:

Connectivity and Trade Agreements: A crucial aspect of the USA's strategy is to promote connectivity among countries in the corridor through infrastructure investments. This includes developing ports, railways, and roads that facilitate the movement of goods, enhance trade, and strengthen economic ties. Simultaneously, the USA aims to negotiate trade agreements that simplify and increase trade among the participating nations.

Digital Connectivity: Recognising the importance of digital infrastructure, the USA intends to support and facilitate the development of high-speed internet connectivity and digital infrastructure networks in the corridor. This digital connectivity will enable enhanced data sharing, e-commerce facilitation, and technological cooperation among the countries involved.

Regional Security and Stability:

Counterterrorism Cooperation: The USA works closely with its partners in the corridor to combat what it calls "terrorism" and address regional security challenges from the American administration's perspective. This cooperative effort includes intelligence sharing, coordinated military operations, and capacity building to promote regional stability and counter potential threats.

Promoting Stability: In addition to the so-called "counterterrorism" efforts, the USA supports initiatives aimed at establishing political stability (which becomes sometimes instability: i.e. Iraq, Libya, Syria, Yemen, etc.) fostering economic growth, and addressing social issues in countries along the corridor. These efforts aim to deter radicalism (but not Israeli extremism), strengthen governance, and promote human rights, ultimately contributing to a more stable and secure region.

Conclusion:

As China's influence expands through the Belt and Road Initiative, the USA's response in the India-Middle East-Europe Corridor reflects its determination to maintain a balance of power and protect its strategic interests. By leveraging partnerships, promoting infrastructure development, and ensuring regional security and stability, the USA asserts its position and provides a counterweight to China's growing dominance.

References and Further Reading:

1. Zimmermann, Nils, and Akshay Mathur. "The Role of India in US Strategic Thinking in the Indo-Pacific." IAI Commentaries, no. 21, (2020): 1-8.

2. Sarkar, Samir. "India, US and the Emerging Indo-Pacific Architecture." Indian Council of World Affairs, 7, no. Special Issue (2018): 118-37.

3. Department of Defense. "Indo-Pacific Strategy Re-

port: Preparedness, Partnerships, and Promoting a Networked Region." US Government, 2019.

4. Chanda, Nayan. "India's Response to China's Belt and Road Initiative." Carnegie Endowment for International Peace, 2017.

5. Singh, Harmeet. "India's Geopolitical Interests in Central Asia and Their Relevance to US Interests." National Bureau of Asian Research, 2019.

6. Hudson, John. "The Impact of the Belt and Road Initiative in the Middle East and North Africa." Middle East Institute, 2019.

7. Karam, Marina, and Giuseppe Dentice. "The Silk Road Economic Belt and the Transatlantic Relationship." Atlantic Council, 2019.

8. Selden, Zachary, and Joseph M. Humire. "China and Latin America: A Strategic Approach to the Belt and Road Initiative." Center for a Secure Free Society, 2018.

9. European Parliament. "EU-China Relations: From Connectivity to Dependence?" Policy Department for External Relations, 2019.

10. Ministry of External Affairs. "India and Asia-Africa Growth Corridor: Perspectives and Prospects." Government of India, 2018.

11. Mohan, C. Raja. "India's Strategic Choices in the Indo-Pacific." Carnegie Endowment for International Peace, 2019.

12. Council on Foreign Relations. "China's Belt and

Road Initiative." Council on Foreign Relations—Independent Task Force Report No. 74, 2019.

13. Mance, Henry. "US and European Allies Seek to Reduce Belt and Road's Global Influence." Financial Times, 2018.

14. Kaplan, Robert D. "Why America Needs the Belt and Road." Foreign Policy, 2018.

15. Blanchard, Jean-Marc F. "China's Belt and Road Initiative: Implications for the Middle East." Center for Strategic and International Studies, 2018.

16. Su, Tsung-chi. "The Contemporary Geopolitics of the US and China's New Silk Road Strategies."

17. Rumer, Eugene B. "Russia and China in the Middle East: The Impact of the Belt and Road Initiative." Carnegie Endowment for International Peace, 2018.

18. Warburg, Gabriel. "The Belt and Road Initiative in Europe: Implications for the European Union and the United States." German Marshall Fund, 2019.

19. Bhardwaj, Prashant. "Great Power Competition and the Belt and Road Initiative: Understanding India's Role." Naval War College Review, vol. 72, no. 4 (2019): 35-54.

20. Auslin, Michael R. "Competing with China: Lessons and Concerns." Hoover Institution, 2019.

21. Burke, Andrew, and Neil Renwick. "US-China Rivalry and the Belt and Road Initiative." Chatham House, 2019.

22. Trenin, Dmitri. "Russia and China: The Belt and

Road Initiative and the Northern Sea Route." Carnegie Endowment for International Peace, 2017.

23. Wenhui, Zhao. "EU-China Relations in the Belt and Road Initiative Context." The Chinese Journal of Global Governance, vol. 4, no. 1 (2018): 3-20.

24. Sutter, Robert G. "The Trump Administration Responds to China's Belt and Road Initiative." The National Bureau of Asian Research, 2018.

25. Swaine, Michael D., et al. "Chinese Influence Activities in Europe: National Responses and Resilience." RAND Corporation, 2018.

26. Noland, Marcus. "Sizing Up China's Belt and Road Initiative: Economic Statecraft, Development, and Governance." Peterson Institute for International Economics, 2018.

27. Kuo, Lily, and Julian Borger. "Europe and China 'take control' of future global internet governance." The Guardian, 2019.

28. Ikenberry, G. John. "The Beijing Consensus and the Crisis of Developmental Liberalism." Foreign Affairs, vol. 87, no. 1 (2008): 23-37.

29. Ye, Min. "Assessing China's Grand Strategy: A Power Cycle Perspective." The Chinese Journal of International Politics, vol. 5, no. 3 (2012): 313-36.

30. Medeiros, Evan. "China's Grand Strategy: Contradictory Foreign Policy Goals." The Washington Quarterly, vol. 26, no. 1 (2002): 7-22.

Chapter 5

Unveiling the Transnational Rail and Port Agreement

The unveiling of the Transnational Rail and Port Agreement marked a seminal moment in the development of global infrastructure. This ambitious endeavour aimed to connect key regions by establishing an integrated network of rail and port infrastructure, fostering economic integration, and promoting cooperation among participating nations. It presented an opportunity to bridge continents, facilitate trade, and enhance the socio-economic development of the involved countries.

The Transnational Rail and Port Agreement emerged from years of painstaking negotiations and meticulous planning. Supported by countries spread across Asia, Europe, and Africa, this initiative is intended to overcome existing logistical and trade barriers by providing a seamless transportation network. By promoting the efficient movement of goods, resources, and people, the agreement sought to unlock tremendous economic potential and promote shared prosperity.

Based on a comprehensive analysis of transport corridors and economic opportunities, the agreement outlined a series of major projects aimed at enhancing connectivity. These encompassed the construction of new rail lines, the modernisation and upgrading of existing infrastructure, and the development of state-of-the-art port facilities. The sheer scale and scope of these projects were intended to create efficient transport corridors, reducing transit times, and increasing trade flows.

One of the key objectives of the Transnational Rail and Port Agreement was to enhance regional economic integration by creating seamless transport links. These efforts aimed to reduce trade costs, enhance competitiveness, and foster closer economic cooperation among participating countries. By establishing reliable and efficient transportation networks, the agreement sought to attract foreign direct investment, promote inter-regional trade, and stimulate economic growth.

The Transnational Rail and Port Agreement placed a strong emphasis on sustainability and environmental responsibility. Incorporating greener technologies and promoting the use of renewable energy sources were vital components of the initiative. This commitment aimed to mitigate the ecological impact of increased trade and transportation, ensuring that economic development was achieved in a sustainable manner. Strategies such as electrification of rail lines, emissions reduction programmes, and the integration of nature-based solutions into port design were considered to minimise the environmental footprint of the infrastructure projects.

Funding for such an immense undertaking was a significant challenge that necessitated extensive negotiations and collaborative efforts. Participating nations engaged in discussions regarding financial contributions and burden-sharing, seeking to allocate resources fairly while ensuring the viability of the projects. Various financial mechanisms, including public-private partnerships, development funds, and international assistance, were explored to generate the necessary capital for implementation. Multilateral development banks, such as the Asian Development Bank and the World Bank, played a crucial role in providing financial support and technical expertise to facilitate project implementation.

Despite the optimism surrounding the Transnational Rail and Port Agreement, concerns and criticisms were voiced from different quarters. Sceptics argued that the mega-project could potentially exacerbate existing inequities, as the benefits might disproportionately favour certain regions. Environmental risks, including deforestation, pollution, and habitat destruction, were also raised as significant issues. Additionally, the potential for disruptive socioeconomic changes and questions of national sovereignty in relation to transnational infrastructure posed further challenges. Stakeholder engagement and comprehensive impact assessments were crucial in addressing these concerns and ensuring that the benefits of the agreement were equitably shared among the participating nations.

Nonetheless, the agreement showcased the ambitions and determination of nations to forge closer ties and reap the benefits of enhanced connectivity. It represented a paradigm shift in global development, marking a new era of integration and collaboration through infrastructure networks. The Transnational Rail and Port Agreement had the potential to alter global trade patterns, reshape regional dynamics, and influence the balance of power in an increasingly interconnected world.

As the agreement moved forward, the world watched with anticipation to see how this ambitious infrastructure network would unfold. Continuous monitoring and evaluation were crucial to assess and manage the impacts and benefits of the agreement. Collaborative efforts among participating nations, civil society, and stakeholders were necessary to address any challenges that arose, ensure transparency, and achieve the desired outcomes. Effective governance structures, clear implementation frameworks, and robust accountability mechanisms were vital to realising the transformative potential of the Transnational Rail and Port Agreement.

References and Further Reading:

1. ADB. (2019). Transnational Transport Corridors in Southeast Asia. Asian Development Bank.
2. World Bank. (2020). Connecting the Coasts: The Transnational Rail and Port Agreement. World Bank Group.
3. UNCTAD. (2018). Trade and Development Report 2018: Power, Platforms, and the Fracturing of Global Trade. United Nations Conference on Trade and Development.

4. IISD. (2021). Sustainable Infrastructure: A Framework and Principles for Project Assessment. International Institute for Sustainable Development.

5. OECD. (2019). Governance Principles for Public Infrastructure: Principles to Enable Sustainable Infrastructure for the Future. Organisation for Economic Co-operation and Development.

6. EIA. (2021). Environmental Impact Assessment Guidelines for Infrastructure Projects. Environmental Impact Assessment Resource and Information Center.

7. Song, Y. (2019). Belt and Road Initiative: Bridging the World through Connectivity, Development, and Cooperation. Journal of Contemporary China, 28(117), 709-716.

8. Li, W., et al. (2020). Assessing the Economic and Environmental Impacts of the Belt and Road Initiative. Energy Economics, 86, 104638.

9. Reis, J., et al. (2019). The Belt and Road Initiative: An Analysis of Regional Disintegration Trends. Journal of Contemporary Asia, 49(2), 310-332.

10. Economist Intelligence Unit. (2018). Belt and Road Initiative: Challenges and Opportunities. Economist Intelligence Unit.

11. Wang, Y., & Wei, F. (2021). Infrastructure Connectivity of China's Belt and Road Initiative. Journal of Comparative Economics, 49(2), 486-503.

Chapter 6

Tactics For Sabotaging China's Belt and Road Initiative

The Belt and Road Initiative (BRI), introduced by China in 2013, represents a monumental effort to bolster connectivity, trade, and economic integration across Asia, Europe, Africa, and beyond. Nevertheless, this ambitious endeavour has encountered determined opposition from a variety of nations and international entities intent on undermining its progress. This chapter delves into the intricate strategies employed to hinder China's BRI and explores the potential repercussions it could have on the global landscape of power dynamics.

1. The Geopolitical Contest

Central to the efforts aimed at sabotaging China's BRI is the overarching geopolitical battle between China and established powers seeking to maintain their strategic dominance. The expansive reach of the BRI has raised concerns about China's increasing influence, igniting fears of a potential shift in the global power dynamic and a waning role for long-standing powers. Importantly, it's noteworthy that a significant majority of countries across Africa, Asia, and South America favour this shift. These nations have little interest in perpetuating a system that emerged in the aftermath of World War II, where a select few nations exerted near-global hegemony in what closely resembled a global dictatorship.In response to the BRI's rise, opposition emanates from both individual nations and collective efforts by international players, with the United States prominently leading the charge to actively subvert China's BRI. The concerns revolve around preserving U .S. strategic dominance, upholding existing alliances, and thwarting China's ascent as a global superpower.

2. Economic Hurdles and Debt Diplomacy

Another strategy employed to obstruct the BRI is to scrutinise the economic viability and sustainability of its projects. Critics argue that Chinese investments in infrastructure often result in unsustainable debt burdens for host nations, rendering them overly reliant on China. They contend that China engages in debt diplomacy by deliberately burdening countries with loans that are difficult to sustain, thereby allowing China to wield economic and political leverage over them (presumably preferring these nations to be indebted to the IMF and major Western corporations, presented as humanitarian benefactors). By spotlighting these concerns and the potential financial risks tied to the BRI, opponents aim to discourage other nations from welcoming Chinese investments.

3. Fomenting Regional Alliances and Discord

Efforts to sabotage China's BRI also encompass the exploitation of regional rivalries and divisions. Nations wary of China's growing influence aim to undermine the initiative by forging alliances with rival powers or supporting separatist movements in regions where infrastructure projects are planned or underway. By stoking tensions and conflicts, adversaries hope to disrupt the smooth implementation of the BRI. These tactics aim to capitalise on existing divisions within regions and leverage historical and territorial disputes to weaken China's sway.

4. Propaganda and Influence Operations

The battle against the BRI extends into the realm of information warfare. Opponents deploy propaganda and influence operations to shape public opinion, both domestically and internationally, against China's initiative. Leveraging diverse media platforms, they accentuate alleged negative impacts of the BRI, such as environmental concerns, labour issues, and cultural imperialism, in a bid to discredit China's efforts and erode support for the initiative. This information warfare seeks to cast doubt on China's intentions, divert attention from their infrastructural accomplishments, and exploit preexisting negative stereotypes.

5. Legal and Regulatory Hurdles

Opponents of the BRI seek to hinder China's progress through legal and regulatory measures. They subject the legal frameworks and agreements underpinning the initiative to intense scrutiny and challenge, with the aim of erecting regulatory barriers and legal obstacles that impede or delay project implementation. Such challenges often centre on concerns regarding transparency, procedural fairness, and environmental sustainability. Critics argue that the absence of accountability and adherence to international standards places local communities and ecosystems at risk.

Conclusion

The campaign to sabotage China's Belt and Road Initiative encompasses multifaceted dimensions, including geopolitical competition, economic impediments, regional rivalries, information warfare, and legal challenges. This comprehensive battle for influence between China and its adversaries is poised to exert far-reaching effects on the future of international relations and the delicate balance of power worldwide.

References and Further Reading:

1. The Geopolitical Battle:

Mahbubani, K. (2018). The Belt and Road Initiative: Reshaping globalisation? Australian Institute of International Affairs.

Paul, T. V. (2020). The United States and China in power transition. National Bureau of Asian Research.

McGregor, R. (2021). The Party: The Secret World of China's Communist Rulers. Harper Business.

2. Economic Obstacles and Debt Diplomacy:

Athukorala, P., & Sen, K. (2021). Assessing debt sustainability under the Belt and Road Initiative. Asian Development Bank Institute.

Kurlantzick, J. (2016). China's ambition in the South China Sea. Council on Foreign Relations.

Griffiths, J. (2021). Belt and Road Initiative: Debt, economics and politics. CNN Business.

3. Perturbing Regional Alliances and Divisions:

Lanteigne, M. (2019). Security implications of the Belt and Road Initiative. Canadian Foreign Policy Journal.

McDermott, R. N., & Baogang, H. (2019). Decoding the security challenges to the Belt and Road Initiative. International Relations of the Asia-Pacific.

Wortzel, L. (2020). Forging New Strategic Relationships: The Impact of China's Belt and Road Initiative. The Jamestown Foundation.

4. Propaganda and Influence Operations:

Kurlantzick J. (2021). The China challenge. Council on Foreign Relations.

Lee K. (2020). The soft power implications of China's Belt and Road Initiative. Journal of Contemporary China.

Mantik D. P. (2021). China's Influence Operations. European Institute for Asian Studies.

5. Legal and Regulatory Challenges:

Wu, S. (2021). Legal challenges faced by the Belt and Road Initiative: examining dispute resolution and investment treaty system. Bulletin of the Transilvania University of Braşov, Series VII: Social Sciences and Law.

Zhang, R. (2020). International legal analysis on the Belt and Road Initiative. Journal of International Trade Law.

Kousantzi, V. (2021). Assessing the environmental impact of China's Belt and Road Initiative (BRI): Challenges and opportunities. Association for the Study of Peak Oil & Gas (ASPO).

Chapter 7

Betting on India to Divide the BRICS

I n this chapter, we examine the concept of dividing the BRICS (Brazil, Russia, India, China, and South Africa) and how the United States strategically bets on India to counter China's influence within the group. This complex global chess game centres around the competing worldviews, economic interests, and geopolitical ambitions of these major powers. Through an in-depth analysis of historical events, policy statements, and expert opinions, we will explore the motivations and implications of the United States' strategic calculations.

1. The BRICS: Background and Significance

The BRICS grouping emerged in 2001, when Goldman Sachs economist Jim O'Neill coined the term to reflect the growing economic influence of Brazil, Russia, India, and China. South Africa joined in 2010, expanding the group's representation across multiple continents. The formation of the BRICS aimed to challenge and coun-terbalance the Western-dominated global order, advocating for reforms that would better reflect the interests of emerging economies.

Initially, the BRICS held great promise as an alternative platform for developing nations to assert their influence and advance their economic agendas. However, over time, divergent interests and visions have strained the unity of the group. While the BRICS have succeeded in establishing their own development bank, called the New Development Bank (NDB), progress on other areas of cooperation, such as the BRICS Business Council and the Contingent Reserve Arrangement, has been limited. These challenges underscore the need for individual BRICS members to reassess their priorities and strategic positioning within the group.

2. Growing Tensions within the BRICS

As the BRICS expanded its scope beyond economics, internal tensions began to surface. One key fault line lies in the differing approaches to economic development and political systems among BRICS members. China's rapid economic rise and its socialist model (in the West, they like to call it "state capitalism", for only capitalism should succeed!) have raised concerns among other members, particularly India. India emphasises democracy, market-based reforms, and a rules-based international system, making it wary of China's assertiveness and its impact on regional stability.

Another flashpoint in BRICS relations is territorial disputes. The longstanding border dispute between India and China, particularly the Doklam standoff in 2017, strained their relationship and highlighted the potential for conflict within the group. This will be exploited by the USA, in the same way it did in the Middle East, pitting Sunnites against Shiites, Christians against Muslims, and Muslims against Jews. Similarly, Russia's problems with Ukraine (largely caused by US political manoeuvring), which led to a short freeze of its membership in the group in 2014, have further complicated the dynamics within the BRICS.

3. The United States and Its Strategic Calculations

Recognising the BRICS' potential to challenge American hegemony, the United States has adopted a multifaceted approach to divide and conquer the group. Diplomatically, the United States seeks to exploit the tensions within the BRICS, offering incentives to align closer with its interests. For instance, the United States has engaged in bilateral strategic dialogues with various BRICS members, such as the US-India Strategic Dialogue, the US-Brazil Strategic Partnership Dialogue, and the US-South Africa Bilateral Commission. These dialogues aim to deepen political, economic, and security cooperation between the United States and individual BRICS members, potentially undermining the group's collective cohesion.

Economically, the United States utilises trade policies and preferential agreements to undermine the collective strength of the BRICS countries. By promoting bilateral trade agreements like the U.S.-India Bilateral Trade and Investment Framework Agreement (BTIFA) and the U. S.-China Phase One Trade Agreement, the United States aims to strengthen economic ties with individual BRICS members while diminishing the group's collective bargaining power. Moreover, the United States engages in military cooperation agreements, primarily with India, as a means to counterbalance China's military expansion in the region. Examples include the US-India Defence Technology and Trade Initiative (DTTI) and the US-India Malabar naval exercises.

4. India's Role and Strategic Positioning

India's rising economic power and growing regional influence have made it an attractive partner for the United States. India's motivations for aligning more closely with the United States include countering China's assertiveness, gaining access to advanced technologies, and fostering economic growth. India aspires to be a global power and sees closer cooperation with the United States as a means to achieve this goal. However, India must navigate careful diplomatic manoeuvring to balance its relations with other BRICS members and address China's response to its alignment with the United States.

India's approach to the BRICS has evolved over time, reflecting its changing priorities and geopolitical considerations. It seeks to leverage the platform to promote equitable global governance, economic cooperation, and sustainable development. However, India's active participation in other regional groupings, such as the Quadrilateral Security Dialogue (Quad) with the United States, Japan, and Australia, underscores its willingness to consider alternative forums to pursue its strategic objectives.

5. Implications for the BRICS and Global Geopolitics

The divisions within the BRICS have far-reaching implications for the group's future cohesion and effectiveness as a unified force. If the United States succeeds in dividing the BRICS, it could weaken the collective bargaining power and influence of the group on the global stage. This fragmentation may lead to the formation of new alliances, realignment of trade flows, and increased tensions among major powers.

China, as the most powerful member of the BRICS, is aware of the United States' strategic calculations and has sought to strengthen its own position within the group. China has proposed initiatives such as the Belt and Road Initiative (BRI) and the Asian Infrastructure Investment Bank (AIIB) to enhance its economic influence and geopolitical clout. By expanding its economic reach and providing infrastructure investments to other BRICS members, China aims to solidify its position as the leading power within the group and counterbalance the United States' influence.

Russia, on the other hand, finds itself in a delicate position within the BRICS due to its strained relations with the United States and its exclusion from the group in 2014. Russia seeks to maintain its influence within the BRICS by emphasising its role as a major energy exporter and leveraging its strategic partnerships with other members, particularly China. However, Russia's geopolitical ambitions and actions, such as its annexation of Crimea, have created tensions within the group, making it more vulnerable to the United States' divide and conquer strategy.

Brazil and South Africa, as the other two members of the BRICS, face their own unique challenges. Brazil is grappling with internal political and economic crises that have hampered its ability to assert itself as a global player. South Africa, meanwhile, confronts domestic socio-economic challenges and struggles to leverage the BRICS platform effectively.

In terms of global geopolitics, a divided BRICS could disrupt the balance of power to the benefit of the USA and create a more fragmented and unpredictable international system. The United States' strategic bet on India and its attempts to weaken the BRICS could lead to a shift in alliances and the formation of new power blocs. This could have implications for global governance, trade patterns, and regional security dynamics.

Furthermore, the BRICS' ability to navigate these challenges and solidify their collective influence will depend on their ability to address internal tensions, find common ground, and present a united front on key global issues. Failure to do so may result in the marginalisation of the BRICS and a diminished role in shaping the global order.

In conclusion, the United States' strategic bet on India to divide the BRICS speaks to the complex dynamics and power struggles in today's multipolar world. The divisions within the BRICS, fuelled by differing interests, visions, and geopolitical ambitions, create opportunities for external actors to exploit and weaken the group. How the BRICS navigate these challenges and assert their collective influence will have significant implications for global geopolitics and the balance of power in the 21st century.

References and Further Reading:

1. The BRICS: Background and Significance:

- O'Neill, Jim. "Building better global economic BRICs." Global Economics Paper No: 66, Goldman Sachs, 2001.

- Ferreira, Claudia, and Barry Gills. "The BRICS region in the global system: Changing contexts." BRICS: An anti-capitalist critique. Pluto Press, 2015.

2. Growing Tensions within the BRICS:

- Pillalamarri, Akhilesh. "Explained: The History of the India-China Border Dispute." The Diplomat, 8 July 2020.

- Lo, Bobo, and Joris Larik. "The Crimean Crisis and International Law: An Appraisal." Ethics & International Affairs, vol. 28, no. 3, 2014, pp. 325–352.

3. The United States and Its Strategic Calculations:

- Bremmer, Ian. "The United States and Russia: Bipolar power in a multipolar world." Challenge to the Hegemon: The United States and Russia in a Changing World Order, 2020, pp. 29-59.

- Zarasul Islam, Muhammad, et al. "The Indo-Pacific Strategy and China's Response." Asian Journal of Political Science, vol. 29, no. 1, 2021, pp. 46-69.

4. India's Role and Strategic Positioning:

- Medcalf, Rory. "How India Sees the World: Kautilya, the Arthashastra and Beyond." Indian Foreign Affairs Journal, vol. 6, no. 3, 2011, pp. 257-279.

- Scott, David, and Anthony Shackleton. "India and the

Contest for Influence in the Indo-Pacific." The Round
Table, vol. 110, no. 1, 2021, pp. 41-53.

Chapter 8

The Strategic Shift of the Gulf Arab Countries Following the US Betrayal

I n recent years, the Gulf Arab countries have embarked on a momentous strategic shift, recalibrating their alliances and redefining their geopolitical position. This chapter examines the factors behind this significant change and explores the implications it has for regional dynamics. By examining their motivations and actions in more depth, we can gain a comprehensive understanding of the momentous transformation occurring in the Gulf.

1. The Rising Influence of Iran

The USA has created a complicated problem between Iran and its Muslim Arab neighbours. For many years since the end of WWII, all the American governments worked to divide Arabs and Persians on an ethnical-religious basis. They encouraged the Shah of Iran to annex three Emirati Islands (Abu Moussa, Tunb al -Kobra, and Tunb al-Sughra), and played the Iranians against the Saudis creating a dangerous fictional rivalry between them — Fictional in the sense that it is empty. The CIA persuaded the leaders of the Gulf Arab countries that Iran was a significant threat to their stability and hegemony in the region. It did the same with Iraq. The goal was at least threefold:

1) Divide and conquer.

2) Sell weapons worth billions of dollars.

3) Create instability through wars to control the oil fields and supplies.

Iran, feeling surrounded by hostile powers, started a quest for regional dominance, coupled with its support for various proxy groups, including the Houthis in Yemen, Shiite militias in Iraq, and Hezbollah in Lebanon, has also created a sense of urgency and a growing need for a strategic shift in approach.

2. The Nuclear Deal and its Aftermath

The signing of the Joint Comprehensive Plan of Action (JCPOA), commonly known as the Iran Nuclear Deal, raised numerous concerns among the Gulf Arab countries. While the agreement aimed to limit Iran's nuclear programme, they feared that it would embolden Iran to further assert its influence in the region. Many Gulf states felt betrayed by their traditional ally, the United States, as they believed the deal did not adequately address their security concerns, including Iran's ballistic missile programme and regional meddling. It was the beginning of the wake up to the reality of their relationship with the USA. They started understanding that when Washington finds a way that serves its interests, the old friends are not considered anymore. That's why they were not consulted about a deal that concerns them directly (their region), but was made behind their backs.

Moreover, the JCPOA resulted in the lifting of economic sanctions on Iran, providing it with a financial windfall that could potentially bolster its support for proxy groups. The Gulf Arab countries, particularly Saudi Arabia and the UAE, viewed this development as a direct threat to their regional interests.

3. Iran's Asymmetric Warfare and Cyber Capabilities

Alongside conventional military tactics, Iran has persistently utilised asymmetric warfare strategies to project power and destabilise its rivals. The Gulf Arab countries have experienced the repercussions of Iran's actions, such as attacks on oil installations, naval harassment, and cyber operations targeting critical infrastructure. Recognising the need to adapt, the Gulf states have sought to enhance their own cyber capabilities and develop regional cooperation to counter Iran's asymmetric tactics.

For example, Saudi Arabia, the UAE, and Bahrain established the Saudi-led Islamic Military Counter Terrorism Coalition (IMCTC) to enhance cooperation and build collective capabilities in countering terrorist groups and Iran-sponsored activities. This coalition serves as a platform for sharing intelligence, conducting joint military exercises, and coordinating efforts to combat terrorism and regional threats.

4. The Impact of Regional Conflicts

The Chaos in Yemen

The ongoing conflict in Yemen has played a pivotal role in catalysing the strategic shift within the Gulf Arab countries. The Houthi rebels, backed by Iran, were perceived as a threat to the stability of Saudi Arabia and the United Arab Emirates (UAE), prompting these nations to intervene militarily in support of the "internationally recognised government"— internationally recognised, only because the USA so decided.

This prolonged engagement in Yemen has imposed substantial economic and human costs on the Gulf states, compelling them to reevaluate their alliances and seek alternative avenues for security.

Furthermore, the conflict has revealed the vulnerabilities of the Gulf Arab countries' security apparatuses, as evidenced by Houthi missile attacks targeting Saudi Arabia's infrastructure. This realisation has fuelled the urgency for greater cooperation and strengthening of defence capabilities, including improved missile defence systems, intelligence sharing, and joint military exercises.

5. The Sectarian Divide and Regional Proxy Wars

The Gulf Arab countries find themselves embroiled in a complex power struggle fuelled by sectarian divisions. The rise of Iran's influence, combined with its support for Shiite militias across the region, has heightened the sectarian tension. Saudi Arabia, as the leader of the "Sunni-majority Gulf states," (Sunni majority is a media label created by the US imperialist "divide and conquer"; Islam is neither Sunni nor Shiite) was "encouraged" to feel particularly threatened by Iran's efforts to project its brand of Shia Islam across the Middle East. This sectarian divide has further intensified the strategic shift and led to deepening rivalries and proxy wars in Bahrain, Iraq, Lebanon, and Syria. It is, as we said, the core of the US strategy in the Middle East to divide all the parties. Otherwise, why should the Saudi government care if there are more Shiite or more Sunnite in the world? Who cares anyway? Shiites and Sunnites are just two sections of the same universal religion. They pray to the same God and follow the same prophet, who was neither Sunni nor Shiite. But the Americans have no interest in seeing the Muslims rise as a united community.

That's why, they will do everything possible to undermine the new relationship between Saudi Arabia and Iran, engineered by the Chinese genius.

Countries like Bahrain have faced internal challenges with Iran's support for Shia opposition groups and the sectarian polarisation that followed the 2011 Arab Spring protests. The Gulf Arab countries view these proxy wars and sectarian conflicts as detrimental to the region's stability, prompting them to seek broader regional and international collaborations to counterbalance Iran's influence.

6. The Role of External Powers

The United States: A Changing Stance and Diminished Reliability

The United States has historically been a crucial ally and security guarantor for the Gulf Arab countries. However, their perception of American commitment has shifted as they witnessed a change in US priorities and a reduced focus on the region. Disillusionment grew with the Obama administration's pursuit of the Iran Nuclear Deal, which was seen as sacrificing regional security interests. The subsequent Trump administration's initial attempts to take a tougher stance were accompanied by a certain level of unpredictability and wavering commitment. As a result, the Gulf states have been forced to reassess their reliance on the US and actively pursue alternative strategic partnerships to protect their interests.

Saudi Arabia, in particular, has sought to diversify its strategic partnerships by strengthening ties with countries like Russia and China. The Kingdom's Crown Prince, Mohammed bin Salman's visits to both countries underscored a desire for expanded economic, military, and diplomatic cooperation beyond the traditional alliances. Similarly, the UAE has sought to deepen its relations with countries like India and France, aiming to ensure its security and economic interests are not solely dependant on the United States.

The Emergence of China and the Pursuit of Economic Diversification

The increasing economic and geopolitical influence of China in the Gulf region has not gone unnoticed by the Gulf Arab countries. As China's demand for energy resources continues to rise, coupled with its investments in infrastructure and trade, the Gulf states have recognised the need to prioritise their relationships with this rising power. Moreover, China's willingness to engage without meddling in regional conflicts has been perceived as beneficial for Gulf states seeking stability and economic diversification. This shift towards China represents a proactive approach to diversifying their alliances and serves as a counterbalance to Iran's influence.

China's Belt and Road Initiative (BRI), which aims to enhance connectivity and trade between Asia, Europe, the Middle East, and Africa, has presented opportunities for the Gulf Arab countries to attract Chinese investments and diversify their economies. This economic cooperation aligns with the Gulf states' aspirations for economic diversification beyond their reliance on oil revenues and presents an alternative avenue for growth and development.

Conclusion:

The strategic shift undertaken by the Gulf Arab countries reflects their resolute determination to safeguard their interests in a rapidly evolving regional landscape. Motivated by Iran's expansionist ambitions, regional conflicts, the changing dynamics of global power, and the increasing need for diversified alliances, these nations are resolutely reevaluating their partnerships and forging new relationships. As the ongoing struggle for influence continues, the Gulf Arab countries remain steadfast in their pursuit of maintaining stability and asserting their presence on the world stage.

References and Further Reading:

1. The Rising Influence of Iran:

Wehrey, Frederic, et al. "Iran's Role in the Arab World." RAND Corporation, 2009.

Gause, F. Gregory III. "Saudi Arabia and Iran: The Struggle to Shape the Middle East." The Middle East Journal, Vol. 72, No. 1, 2018.

2. The Nuclear Deal and its Aftermath:

Parsi, Trita. "Losing an Enemy: Obama, Iran, and the Triumph of Diplomacy." Yale University Press, 2017.

Al-Tamimi, Naser. "Gulf States and Iran: A Complex and Changing Relationship." Middle East Policy, Vol. XXI, No. 4, Winter 2014.

3. Iran's Asymmetric Warfare and Cyber Capabilities:

Knights, Michael. "Iran's Military Effectiveness on Land." Strategic Studies Institute, US Army War College, 2017.

Bronk, Chris. "Cyber Threats and Gulf Arab States." The James A. Baker III Institute for Public Policy, Rice University, 2013.

4. The Impact of Regional Conflicts:

Salisbury, Peter. "Yemen: National Chaos, Local Order." Chatham House, 2017.

Bapat, Navin A., and Bo Ram Kwon. "When are Sanctions Effective? A Bargaining and Enforcement Framework." International Organization, Vol. 69, No. 1, 2015.

5. The Sectarian Divide and Regional Proxy Wars:

Wehrey, Frederic. "Sectarian Politics in the Gulf: From the Iraq War to the Arab Uprisings." Columbia University Press, 2014.

Matthiesen, Toby. "Sectarian Gulf: Bahrain, Saudi Arabia, and the Arab Spring That Wasn't." Stanford University Press, 2013.

6. The Role of External Powers:

Jones, Toby Craig, and Nicholas B. Breyfogle. "America, Oil, and War in the Middle East." The Journal of American History, Vol. 99, No. 1, 2012.

Scobell, Andrew, and Nader, Alireza. "China in the Middle East: The Wary Dragon." RAND Corporation, 2016.

Conclusion:

Kamrava, Mehran. "The International Politics of the Persian Gulf." Routledge, 2012.

Gause, F. Gregory III. "The Future of U.S.-Saudi Relations: The Kingdom and the Power." Foreign Affairs, July/August 2016 Issue.

Chapter 9

Regaining Control - The USA's Influence over Saudi Arabia and the UAE

The United States, faced with the growing assertiveness of China's Belt and Road Initiative and the shifting dynamics in global power, has been actively strategizing to regain its influence in key regions, particularly over countries vital to its national interests. Among these countries, Saudi Arabia and the United Arab Emirates (UAE) hold a prominent position due to their economic prowess and geostrategic significance in the Middle East. How the USA has been working to reclaim control over these Gulf Arab nations, employing a combination of economic incentives, military cooperation, political manoeuvring, and cultural influence, is our focus in this chapter.

Economic Leverage and Arms Sales

The USA has historically maintained strong ties with Saudi Arabia and the UAE, driven largely by their immense oil wealth and shared opposition to regional adversaries. However, in recent years, China's economic enticements have threatened to undermine America's long-standing dominance in the region. In response, the USA has taken a proactive approach, utilising its economic leverage to secure lucrative arms sales to these Gulf nations.

The United States has become a major arms supplier to Saudi Arabia and the UAE, with multi-billion dollar deals for advanced weaponry and military technology. These sales not only bolster the military capabilities of these countries but also ensure their dependence on American technology, spare parts, and support. By establishing this reliance, the USA strengthens its control over their defence sectors and enhances their interoperability with American forces.

Securing Energy Cooperation Deals

Recognising the vital importance of energy resources, the USA has sought to maintain a firm grip on the Gulf Arab countries. Through astute negotiations and leveraging its technological expertise, the USA has successfully secured lucrative energy cooperation deals with Saudi Arabia and the UAE.

In Saudi Arabia, the United States has worked closely with the government to modernise and diversify its energy sector. This includes providing expertise in hydrocarbon exploration, refining, and petrochemicals production, as well as facilitating knowledge exchange and collaboration in renewable energy projects. By positioning themselves as a strategic partner, the USA maintains a significant role in Saudi Arabia's energy landscape, ensuring a steady supply of oil and safeguarding their interests.

Similarly, in the UAE, the United States has forged

strong ties in the energy sector. The UAE has embarked on an ambitious path to reduce its dependency on oil and foster sustainable energy sources. The USA has actively supported the implementation of renewable energy projects, encouraging partnerships between American and Emirati companies in solar, wind, and nuclear energy. These collaborations serve to strengthen the United States' influence over the UAE's energy transition, ensuring their involvement in key projects and shaping the country's energy policies in alignment with American interests.

Political Manoeuvring and Diplomatic Pressure

Asserting its dominance in the region, the USA has engaged in proactive political manoeuvring to ensure its influence over Saudi Arabia and the UAE. By leveraging its extensive political and diplomatic networks, the United States has cultivated close ties with key decision-makers, exerting pressure to align their policies with American interests.

In Saudi Arabia, the United States strategically leverages its alliances to influence regional conflicts and shape outcomes that align with their objectives. The close cooperation between the two countries on issues such as countering Iran's influence, combating "terrorism", and "resolving" conflicts in the Middle East (without resolving any) solidifies the US-Saudi relationship. By actively engaging in diplomatic efforts, the USA ensures its voice is heard and its recommendations considered in regional affairs, further cementing their position of influence.

Similarly, in the UAE, the United States has nurtured strong political ties. The two nations collaborate on countering extremism, enhancing security cooperation, and promoting stability in the region. The presence of American military bases and the establishment of joint defence agreements, such as the Strategic Cooperation Agreement, significantly contribute to the United States' ability to exert its influence in the country's political landscape.

Countering Chinese Investments and Disrupting Regional Economics

China's Belt and Road Initiative, aimed at promoting economic connectivity and infrastructure development, has encroached upon traditional American territories of influence, including the Gulf Arab states. In a provocative move to counter Chinese investments, the USA has partnered with regional "allies" to launch projects and initiatives that compete directly with China's economic endeavours.

The United States, in coordination with Saudi Arabia and the UAE, has established alternative investment opportunities to disrupt Chinese plans and regain its economic control. These efforts only aim to undermine China's influence. By encouraging joint ventures in various industries, fostering entrepreneurship and innovation, and facilitating the growth of small and medium-sized enterprises, the USA seems working to "support" the Gulf nations' economic diversification away from oil dependency. Such diversification efforts strengthen the countries' resilience and autonomy while simultaneously reducing their vulnerability to external pressures, excluding the American.

Cultural Influence and Soft Power

Recognising the power of cultural influence and soft

power, the USA has also employed various means to shape the perception and values of the societies in Saudi Arabia and the UAE. Through cultural and educational exchange programmes, scholarships, and partnerships, the United States actively promotes its language, values, way of life and ideology still repelled in those conservative countries.

American universities and cultural institutions, always in quest of funding, have established branches or collaborations in Saudi Arabia and the UAE, under the pretension of transferring knowledge, ideas, and values. Through these academic and cultural exchanges, the United States seeks to foster a deeper understanding of American ideals, strengthen people-to-people ties, influence the direction of social and cultural norms, and shape the minds of young generations. By promoting American education and cultural experiences, the USA cultivates a sense of familiarity among Saudi and Emirati citizens, amplifying its soft power in the region.

Conclusion:

Through a combination of economic incentives, military cooperation, political manoeuvring, and cultural influence, the United States seeks to regain its dominance and influence over Saudi Arabia and the UAE, countering the growing assertiveness of China's Belt and Road Initiative. This provocative battle for control needs time, energy and funds to reshape the geopolitical landscape of the Middle East and the Gulf region, with significant implications for global power dynamics. As tensions escalate, the world watches with bated breath to see whether the USA can succeed in reclaiming its hold over these vital nations and solidify its position as a leading global power. But the unstoppable rise of China may make all those efforts a waste of time.

References and Further Reading:

Economic Leverage and Arms Sales

Blanchard, Christopher M. "Arms Sales in the Middle East: Trends and Analytical Perspectives for U.S. Policy." Congressional Research Service, 2020.

Riedel, Bruce. "Kings and Presidents: Saudi Arabia and the United States Since FDR." Brookings Institution Press, 2018.

Securing Energy Cooperation Deals

Krane, Jim. "Energy Kingdoms: Oil and Political Survival in the Persian Gulf." Columbia University Press,

2019.

O'Sullivan, Meghan L. "Windfall: How the New Energy Abundance Upends Global Politics and Strengthens America's Power." Simon & Schuster, 2017.

Political Manoeuvring and Diplomatic Pressure

Indyk, Martin S., et al. "Bending History: Barack Obama's Foreign Policy." Brookings Institution Press, 2012.

House, Karen Elliott. "On Saudi Arabia: Its People, Past, Religion, Fault Lines - and Future." Knopf, 2012.

Countering Chinese Investments and Disrupting Regional Economics

Rolland, Nadège. "China's Eurasian Century? Political and Strategic Implications of the Belt and Road Initiative." National Bureau of Asian Research, 2017.

Scobell, Andrew, and Nader, Alireza. "China in the Middle East: The Wary Dragon." RAND Corporation, 2016.

Cultural Influence and Soft Power

Nye, Joseph S. "Soft Power: The Means to Success in World Politics." PublicAffairs, 2004.

Zweiri, Mahjoob, and Zahid Shahab Ahmed, eds. "Culture, Soft Power, and the Politics of Middle East Identity." I.B. Tauris, 2019.

Conclusion

Gause, F. Gregory III. "The International Relations of the Persian Gulf." Cambridge University Press, 2010.

Layne, Christopher. "The Peace of Illusions: American

Grand Strategy from 1940 to the Present." Cornell University Press, 2006.

Chapter 10

Obstructing China's Projects in the Middle East

As the battle for global influence intensifies, one region that has become a battleground for geopolitical rivalries is the Middle East. China's ambitious Belt and Road Initiative has extended its reach into this strategically important region, raising concerns among certain actors who aim to obstruct China's projects. In this extended chapter, we will delve deeper into the efforts made to undermine China's growing influence in the Middle East, presenting a comprehensive analysis of the tactics employed by various actors to counter China's expansion.

Unmasking China's Hidden Agenda

The Dragon's Shadow: China's growing presence in the Middle East.

A combination of economic and strategic factors are driving China's growing involvement in the Middle East. Seeking to secure energy resources and expand its market access, China has invested heavily in infrastructure projects and established strategic partnerships with key countries in the region. While Beijing claims that its intentions are purely economic, Western concerns have arisen regarding China's long-term political influence and its potential to engender dependency among nations in the Middle East.

Economic Dominance

China's Belt and Road Initiative serves as a vehicle for

expanding its economic know-how in the Middle East. Through infrastructure investments, China aims to enhance regional connectivity, creating a network of transportation routes that will facilitate the flow of goods and resources. By securing energy supply chains and establishing trade corridors, China seeks to ensure a sustainable shared future and position itself as an indispensable economic partner for Middle Eastern nations.

Implications for the USA and its regional relays:

China's growing influence in the Middle East poses challenges to traditional actors in the region, including the United States and its regional relays like Israel. Beijing's economic allure, coupled with its non-interventionist stance, provides an alternative to the Western model of engagement, potentially diminishing the influence of these actors. As China deepens its involvement in the Middle East, traditional powers find themselves compelled to obstruct China's projects to safeguard their interests and preserve their strategic influence.

Unleashing Geopolitical Manoeuvres

United States: The superpower's covert moves to counter China's projects.

The United States perceives China's expansion in the Middle East as a challenge to its global supremacy. In response, it has employed various covert tactics to counter China's projects. Leveraging its military alliances in the region, particularly with countries like Saudi Arabia and Israel, the US maintains a strategic advantage and exerts pressure on China. It has also utilised economic tools, such as imposing sanctions, initiating trade wars, and discouraging partnerships, to hinder China's progress in the Middle East.

Leveraging Military Alliances: How the US uses its presence in the Middle East as a strategic advantage.

The US capitalises on its military presence in the Middle East to leverage its partnerships and obstruct China's expansion. By maintaining military bases, conducting joint exercises, and providing security cooperation, the US strengthens its alliances with key regional actors. Through these alliances, it can limit China's influence and ensure that its presence is not overshadowed by China's growing economic prowess.

Economic Pressure: Sanctions and trade wars as tools to obstruct China's progress.

Economic pressure tactics, such as sanctions and trade wars, have been used by the US to counter China's projects in the Middle East. By imposing financial restrictions and trade barriers, the US aims to undermine China's economic partnerships and disrupt its supply chains. Through these measures, the US seeks to discourage Middle Eastern countries from deepening their engagement with China and potentially shift their alliances back towards the United States.

Allying with Regional Powers: How the US builds alliances to counter China's influence.

To counter China's growing influence in the Middle East, the US has strengthened partnerships with regional powers. By forging closer ties with countries like Saudi Arabia and the UAE , the US not only bolsters its military presence but also gives the false impression of aligning its interests with these actors who are supposed to have common concerns about China's expanding footprint. Delusional assumption. But who knows? Sometimes fiction works. Cooperating with regional powers makes the US believe that to jointly obstruct China's projects and ensure that its influence remains intact in the region.

India's Strategic Calculus: Why India aims to impede China's projects in the Middle East.

India, too, has begun to perceive China's presence in the Middle East as a challenge. As an emerging power in the Indo-Pacific region, India seeks to assert itself and impede China's projects in the Middle East for several reasons.

The Indo-Pacific Game: Understanding India's desire for a larger role in the region.

India's strategic interests in the Middle East stem from its aspiration to be a key player in the Indo-Pacific region. Recognising the linkages between the Indian Ocean and the Middle East, India aims to establish its influence as a counterweight to China's growing dominance. By obstructing China's projects in the Middle East, India can position itself as a credible alternative and assert its role as a prominent regional power.

Countering Chinese Investments: India's economic alternatives to undermine China's projects.

India, wary of the economic dependency that may result from Chinese investments, has sought to undermine China's projects in the Middle East by providing alternative economic opportunities. By promoting its initiatives such as the International North-South Transport Corridor and the Chabahar Port in Iran, India offers alternative connectivity options to Middle Eastern nations. This allows India to divert attention away from China's projects and presents itself as a reliable economic partner.

Leveraging Historical Ties: How India taps into its historical connections for strategic advantage.

India's historical ties with the Middle East provide a basis for India to leverage its relationships with various countries in the region. By leveraging cultural and historical connections, India aims to build stronger partnerships with countries such as Saudi Arabia, the UAE, and Israel. Through these alliances, India can align its interests with those of regional powers and jointly counter China's projects in the Middle East.

Proxy Battles Unleashed

Saudi Arabia and the United Arab Emirates: Balancing relations between China and the West.

Saudi Arabia and the United Arab Emirates (UAE) find themselves in a delicate balancing act between their economic ties with China and their longstanding relationships with the United States and other Western powers. The Americans assume that as key regional powers, Saudi Arabia and the United Arab Emirates navigate the complexities of managing their strategic partnerships while cautiously countering China's growing influence.

Oil vs. Ideology: Saudi Arabia's hypothetical dilemma in obstructing China's projects.

The Americans assume that Saudi Arabia, as a significant oil exporter, faces a dilemma in obstructing China's projects in the Middle East. While the Kingdom seeks to balance its relationship with China, acknowledging the importance of Chinese energy demand, it also recognises the potential risks of over-dependence. Therefore, Saudi Arabia cautiously approaches China's projects, ensuring that its interests in the region are not compromised.

The UAE's Hypothetical Dual Game: Balancing economic partnerships while countering China's influence.

In the American perspective, it is assumed that the UAE adopts a similar approach to Saudi Arabia, maintaining a dual game : i.e. Balancing economic partnerships while countering China's influence.

The UAE, with its strong economic ties to China, faces hypothetically a similar balancing act. As one of China's largest trading partners in the Middle East, the UAE has benefited greatly from Chinese investments in various sectors, including infrastructure, real estate, and telecommunications. However, the UAE also recognises the need to counter China's growing influence in the region to protect its own strategic interests and maintain its relationships with Western powers. So the American believe. The UAE strategically engages in partnerships with international actors, particularly the United States, to ensure its influence and mitigate the potential risks of Chinese dominance in the Middle East.

Israel's Strategic Calculus: Managing relations with China and the United States.

Israel, a key player in the Middle East, finds itself in a unique position in managing its relations with both China and the United States. While it shares growing economic and technological ties with China, Israel is also heavily reliant on the United States for military and diplomatic support. As such, Israel must carefully navigate its relationships to counter China's expanding influence in the region.

Technological Cooperation: Balancing economic benefits and security concerns.

Israel's technological cooperation with China has been a major driver of their growing economic ties. Chinese companies have invested heavily in Israeli startups, particularly in the tech sector, providing Israel with significant economic benefits. However, concerns have arisen over potential technology transfers and security risks. Israel must carefully assess the economic benefits against the security concerns and work to safeguard its own technological advancements while countering China's projects in the Middle East.

Aligning with the United States: Maintaining strategic partnerships to counter China's influence.

Given its strong alliance with the United States, Israel has been cautious in its engagement with China to avoid jeopardising its relationship with its primary ally. Israel has aligned itself closely with the United States in countering Chinese influence in the Middle East, particularly through joint endeavours in areas such as cybersecurity and intelligence cooperation. By leveraging its strong relationship with the United States, Israel aims to obstruct China's projects and maintain its position as a key regional player.

Countering China's Narrative

The US and India: Diminishing China's soft power in the Middle East.

Both the United States and India recognise the importance of countering China's soft power and narrative-building efforts in the Middle East. China has actively sought to promote its model of development and governance as an alternative to Western influence, eroding the dominance of the United States' narrative in the region. The US and India, therefore, focus on highlighting the drawbacks of China's approach and offering a contrasting narrative to undermine China's influence.

Exposing Human Rights Abuses: Highlighting China's record to undercut its soft power.

The US and India aim to propagate and exaggerate the myth about China's human rights abuses, particularly in Western China and its treatment of Uighur Muslims. By shedding light on China's fictional record, both countries seek to diminish China's soft power in the region and erode its credibility as a model for development and governance. This exposes the "contradictions" between China's narrative and its actions, allowing the US and India to counter China's influence more effectively. How about the real contradictions between American proclaimed values and the let-go genocide in Gaza?

Promoting "Democratic Values": Offering an alternative narrative to challenge China.

Nobody in our time still believe the myth of America as the leader of freedom, democracy and human rights. For the past 78 years, the USA committed a number of crimes against people on all continents that make its pretensions void and nonsensical. Starting with Vietnam, Cambodia, Laos, et ending with the green light to Netanyahu to kill thousands of Palestinians, nobody in our world wants to hear this old song anymore.

Both the United States and India can emphasise democratic values and institutions, positioning themselves as promoters of freedom, human rights, and good governance. The USA has no remaining credibility in the countries of the South. India may lose what remains of its own inheritance from Ghandi and Nehru, by following the USA on the path of demagogy.

Conclusion:

As China's influence in the Middle East expands through its Belt and Road Initiative, various actors are employing strategies to obstruct China's projects and ensure the preservation of their own interests. The United States leverages its military alliances, economic pressure tactics, and regional partnerships to counter China's influence, while India seeks to establish itself as a credible alternative and undermine China's progress through economic initiatives and leveraging historical connections. Regional powers like Saudi Arabia, the UAE, and Israel grapple with the delicate task of balancing economic ties with China while, assumedly, countering its growing influence, according to the US sources. Additionally, the United States and India focus on countering China's soft power by highlighting fictional human rights abuses and promoting American values. As the geopolitical rivalry intensifies, the contest for influence in the Middle East continues, with China's projects facing increasing obstruction from various quarters.

References and Further Reading:

Unmasking China's Hidden Agenda
1. Scobell, Andrew, and Nader, Alireza. "China in the Middle East: The Wary Dragon." RAND Corporation, 2016.

2. Rolland, Nadège. "China's Eurasian Century? Political and Strategic Implications of the Belt and Road Initiative." National Bureau of Asian Research, 2017.

Unleashing Geopolitical Manoeuvres
1. Medeiros, Evan S. "China's International Behavior: Activism, Opportunism, and Diversification." RAND Corporation, 2009.

2. Pant, Harsh V. "India's Foreign Policy: Coping with the Changing World." Orient Blackswan, 2019.

Proxy Battles Unleashed

    1. Cordesman, Anthony H. "Saudi Arabia: National Security in a Troubled Region." Praeger Security International, 2009.

    2. Freilich, Chuck. "Israeli National Security: A New Strategy for an Era of Change." Oxford University Press, 2018.

Countering China's Narrative

    1. Nye, Joseph S. "Soft Power: The Means to Success in World Politics." PublicAffairs, 2004.

    2. Roth, Kenneth. "The Struggle for a New Global Human Rights Norm." Human Rights Watch, 2020.

Conclusion

    1. Kamrava, Mehran. "The International Politics of the Persian Gulf." Routledge, 2012.

    2. Blackwill, Robert D., and Harris, Jennifer M. "War by Other Means: Geoeconomics and Statecraft." Belknap Press, 2016.

Chapter 11

The Impact on Arab Division and the Role of Israel and the CIA

In this chapter, the focus is on the complex dynamics that have led to the division among Arab nations and how Israel has strategically capitalised on these circumstances to enhance its regional influence. The conflict-ridden history of the Middle East has created a fertile ground for external actors to exploit existing fault lines. The purpose of this chapter is to shed light on the impact of Arab division and explore the intriguing role played by Israel in this maelstrom.

Historical Factors Contributing to Arab Division

The division among Arab nations can be traced back to a variety of historical factors. Colonialism played a significant role in shaping the modern Arab states, with European powers drawing borders arbitrarily and fuelling political rivalries. The collapse of the Ottoman Empire further exacerbated tensions as various groups sought to fill the power vacuum. Sectarian differences, exploited by the USA, such as the Sunni-Shia divide, have also contributed to Arab division, as competing religious authorities have vied for influence. Additionally, the Arab world has experienced a history of decentralised governance, with tribal and sectarian loyalties often superseding national identity. These historical legacies, were used by foreign imperialist powers, to create a fragmented political landscape susceptible to external manipulation.

Proxy Conflicts and the Arab Cold War

During the Cold War era, the Arab world became a battleground for proxy conflicts between the United States and the Soviet Union. The intense competition between these superpowers fuelled divisions among Arab nations as they aligned themselves with one side or the other. Egypt, under the leadership of Gamal Abdel Nasser, emerged as the champion of Arab nationalism, advocating for pan-Arab unity and opposing Western imperialism. Meanwhile, countries like Saudi Arabia and Jordan aligned with the United States, seeking to preserve their monarchies and protect their interests.

The Arab Cold War deepened divisions among Arab states, creating a fractured landscape with varying degrees of political, economic, and military alignment. The conflicts in Yemen, Lebanon, and Iraq became proxy theatres, where regional powers and their allies supported opposing factions to gain influence and control. The inter-Arab rivalries, fuelled by external actors, further weakened Arab unity and created a breeding ground for internal conflicts.

Arab-Israeli Conflict and Arab Unity

The ongoing Arab-Israeli conflict has been a central factor in exacerbating Arab division. Following Israel's establishment in 1948, Arab nations saw the newly formed state as an existential threat. They attempted to unify against Israel in various armed conflicts, including the 1948 Arab-Israeli War, the Six-Day War in 1967, and the

Yom Kippur War in 1973. However, these conflicts did not lead to a united Arab front. Instead, they highlighted internal power struggles and rivalries within the Arab world, fuelling further divisions.

The failure to achieve a decisive victory against Israel deeply weakened Arab unity. Some Arab nations, such as Egypt and Jordan, opted for peace treaties with Israel, further fragmenting the Arab stance on the Palestinian cause. The establishment of the Palestinian Liberation Organisation (PLO) presented a potential platform for Arab solidarity, but differing approaches and priorities among Arab states hindered cohesive action. Some countries began prioritising bilateral relations with Israel, leading to divisions within the Arab League. The rise of Islamism in the region also complicated the situation, with groups like Hamas challenging traditional Arab leadership and advocating a more confrontational approach towards Israel.

Israel's Strategic Exploitation of Arab Division: The CIA scored

Israel has skillfully exploited Arab divisions to further its own strategic objectives and enhance its regional influence. Through its intelligence agencies, such as Mossad,

Israel has conducted covert operations within Arab countries, exacerbating existing rivalries and deepening divisions. Mossad's influence has extended beyond espionage and sabotage, as it has cultivated relationships with dissident groups and facilitated their rise to power in certain countries. The divide and conquer strategy employed by Israeli intelligence has been successful in neutralising threats and maintaining a favourable regional balance of power.

Furthermore, Israel, with the US unconditional support, has effectively leveraged its military superiority and technological advancements to solidify its position in the region. Collaborating with some Arab governments, particularly those that share concerns over Iran's regional ambitions (as suggested by the CIA), Israel has formed discreet alliances that have reshaped regional dynamics. These covert alliances, often centred around security and intelligence sharing, have allowed Israel to forge common interests with Arab states, thereby weakening the traditional Arab consensus against Israel.

Consequences for Arab Unity and the Palestinian Cause

The deep-seated divisions among Arab nations have had far-reaching consequences for regional unity and the Palestinian cause. Arab unity, once a beacon of hope for mass movements and collective action, has suffered as governments, advised by the CIA, pursued their own interests rather than a unified Arab vision. This lack of unity has not only hindered efforts to address regional challenges but has also left Arab nations vulnerable to external interference and exploitation.

The Palestinian cause, once at the forefront of Arab unity and activism, has become marginalised amidst broader Arab divisions. The once-central issue has been overshadowed by competing regional interests, internal strife, and geopolitical shifts. The fragmentation of Arab countries' priorities and strategies has limited their effectiveness in aiding the Palestinian cause and finding a just and lasting solution to the Israeli-Palestinian conflict. Moreover, divisions have allowed Israel to expand its settlements in the occupied territories and solidify its control, presenting new challenges for a future Palestinian state.

Conclusion:

The impact of Arab division and the intricate role of

Israel and the CIA in this divide have shaped the Middle East's geopolitical landscape in profound ways. Historical factors, external interventions, and the Arab-Israeli conflict have deepened divisions within the Arab world. Israel's strategic exploitation of these divisions has allowed it to enhance its influence and pursue its own objectives. However, the consequences for regional unity and the Palestinian cause are significant, hindering collective efforts and undermining the prospects for stability and peace in the Middle East. Understanding these dynamics is crucial in formulating strategies that can foster regional cooperation, address the challenges facing the Arab world, and reinvigorate efforts towards a comprehensive resolution to the Israeli-Palestinian conflict.

References and Further Reading:

Historical Factors Contributing to Arab Division:
Anderson, Lisa. "The State and Social Transformation in Tunisia and Libya, 1830-1980." Princeton University Press, 1986.

Quataert, Donald. "The Ottoman Empire, 1700-1922." Cambridge University Press, 2005.

Proxy Conflicts and the Arab Cold War:

Barnett, Michael N. "Dialogues in Arab Politics: Negotiations in Regional Order." Columbia University Press, 1998.

Lesch, David W. "The Middle East and the United States: History, Politics, and Ideologies." Westview Press, 2013.

Arab-Israeli Conflict and Arab Unity:

Segev, Tom. "1967: Israel, the War, and the Year that Transformed the Middle East." Metropolitan Books, 2007.

Tessler, Mark. "A History of the Israeli-Palestinian Conflict." Indiana University Press, 1994.

Israel's Strategic Exploitation of Arab Division:

Bar-Joseph, Uri. "The Watchman Fell Asleep: The Surprise of Yom Kippur and Its Sources." SUNY Press, 2005.

Katz, Yaakov. "The Weapon Wizards: How Israel Became a High-Tech Military Superpower." St. Martin's Press, 2017.

Consequences for Arab Unity and the Palestinian Cause:

Lynch, Marc. "The New Arab Wars: Uprisings and Anarchy in the Middle East." PublicAffairs, 2016.

Khalidi, Rashid. "The Iron Cage: The Story of the Palestinian Struggle for Statehood." Beacon Press, 2006.

Conclusion:

Milton-Edwards, Beverley. "Contemporary Politics in

the Middle East." Polity, 2018.

Telhami, Shibley, and Barnett, Michael. "Identity and Foreign Policy in the Middle East." Cornell University Press, 2002.

Chapter 12

Conclusion and Keyfindings

As we reach the end of this journey into the battle for global influence, we are compelled to delve deeper into the potential outcomes of the transnational rail and port agreement. The implications of this ambitious endeavour may have a chance to shape the future of global geopolitics if China and its allies do not react.

Summarising the Potential Outcomes of the Agreement

The transnational rail and port agreement, with its bold

vision and vast infrastructure plans, has set the stage for a new era of competition between China's Belt and Road Initiative and the USA's countermove, the India-Middle East-Europe Corridor. This clash of titans has already ignited a fierce struggle for supremacy, with each side manoeuvring its pieces strategically on the geopolitical chessboard.

The battle lines are drawn, and the stakes could not be higher. The potential outcomes of this clash are vast and varied, with far-reaching consequences that will reverberate through every corner of the globe. Will China's Belt and Road Initiative dominate the global economic landscape, cementing its place as the world's leading superpower? Or will the USA succeed in obstructing and undermining China's projects, reclaiming its position as the unrivalled global influencer?

Exploring the Potential Implications

1. Geopolitical Balance: The battle for influence between China and the USA presents a profound shift in the global balance of power. As China's Belt and Road Initiative aims to increase its economic and political sway across continents, the USA's countermove seeks to maintain its traditional dominance. The outcome of this struggle will shape the geopolitical landscape for years to come.

China's ambitious Belt and Road Initiative is an unprecedented attempt to extend its influence globally. By connecting countries through a vast network of infrastructure projects, including railways, ports, pipelines, and highways, China aims to boost trade and foster economic integration. This ambitious initiative seeks to expand its political influence in regions like Asia, Africa, Europe, and even the Americas.

On the other hand, the USA's countermove, the India-Middle East-Europe Corridor, aims to counterbalance China's growing influence and safeguard American interests. This corridor envisions strengthening economic cooperation between the USA, India, and countries in the Middle East and Europe. By leveraging its relationships and resources in these regions, the USA aims to maintain its status as the world's leading superpower.

2. Diplomatic Alliances: The pursuit of influence in the Middle East, a pivotal battleground, has led to complex diplomatic reshuffling. Both China and the USA have sought alliances with Arab nations, aiming to secure strategic access to crucial resources and leverage their geopolitical agendas. This game of alliances adds layers of complexity to the already intricate web of global diplomacy.

China's Belt and Road Initiative has found willing partners in countries like Iran, Saudi Arabia, and the United Arab Emirates. These nations welcome China's investments in infrastructure and see the initiative as an opportunity for economic growth. Meanwhile, the USA has sought to strengthen traditional alliances in the Middle East, ensuring that countries like Israel, Saudi Arabia, and Egypt remain firmly within its sphere of influence.

Political and security considerations, in addition to economic interests, are driving this alliance-building conflict. Arab states carefully navigate their relationships with China and the USA, seeking to extract maximum benefits while managing the risks associated with supporting one side over the other.

3. Economic Integration: The transnational rail and port agreement's primary focus on infrastructure development highlights how economic integration is becoming a key tool in the pursuit of global influence. By enhancing transport connectivity and facilitating trade, China and the USA strive to solidify their economic ties and expand their spheres of influence.

China's Belt and Road Initiative aims to create a vast network of infrastructure projects that connect countries along ancient trade routes. By improving transport infrastructure, China seeks to reduce barriers to trade, increase market access, and enhance economic cooperation. This ambitious endeavour has the potential to reshape global trade patterns and increase China's economic dominance.

In response, the USA's India-Middle East-Europe Corridor focuses on enhancing existing connections and establishing new trade routes. By strengthening economic integration between India, the Middle East, and Europe, the USA aims to diversify its economic partnerships and reduce its dependence on any single region. This strategy seeks to safeguard American economic interests while countering China's influence.

4. Technological Dominance: Beyond infrastructure, the battle for global influence also encompasses technological advancements. China's emphasis on emerging technologies such as 5G networks, artificial intelligence, and digital connectivity through the Digital Silk Road has positioned it as a potential leader in the Fourth Industrial Revolution. Meanwhile, the USA seeks to preserve its technological dominance by implementing strategies to protect sensitive technologies and thwart China's advancements.

China's rapid advancements in emerging technologies present both opportunities and challenges for its global influence. With the world's largest market and its drive for innovation, China aims to become a global leader in areas such as 5G networks and artificial intelligence. Through its Digital Silk Road, China also aims to establish itself as a digital hub, connecting nations through digital infrastructure and expanding its technological influence.

Recognising the significance of technology, the USA has adopted a defensive stance to protect its technological advantage. The USA has implemented policies to safeguard critical technologies, strengthen export controls, and scrutinise foreign investments in sensitive industries. Additionally, the USA is actively seeking to foster alliances and partnerships in the technology sector to counter China's growing influence in emerging technologies.

Forecasting Potential Scenarios

While predicting the outcome of this geopolitical tug-of-war is challenging, it is worth considering potential scenarios that may emerge from the transnational rail and port agreement:

1. Scenario One: China's Dominance - If China's Belt and Road Initiative successfully gains traction and overcomes challenges, it could solidify its position as the global economic leader, influencing geopolitical dynamics as well. This scenario could reshape global trade patterns, alliances, and even international institutions.

2. Scenario Two: US Resurgence - Conversely, the USA's India-Middle East-Europe Corridor may gain momentum and emerge as a formidable counterweight to China's ambitions. The USA's strategy could undermine China's efforts, leading to a potential resurgence of American dominance in global affairs.

3. Scenario Three: Multipolar World Order - It is also possible that a balance of power could emerge, with multiple global powers asserting their influence regionally and globally. This scenario could lead to a fragmenting world order, where alliances and relationships become more fluid and complex.

4. Scenario Four: Collaboration and Cooperation - A less adversarial approach could see China and the USA finding areas of collaboration and cooperation, recognising the benefits of shared interests in a rapidly changing world. Such a scenario could lead to a more constructive global order, with mutual benefits for all involved.

Final Thoughts on the Evolving Global Geopolitical Landscape

As the dust settles on this complex game of geopolitical chess, we are left with one undeniable truth – the global landscape is changing. The world is witnessing a shift in power like never before, with long-established alliances being tested, and new players emerging onto the scene. The implications of this battle for global influence extend far beyond economics and infrastructure; they shape the very fabric of international relations and the balance of power across the geopolitical spectrum.

The choices made by nations and entities as they navigate this treacherous terrain will have far-reaching consequences for generations to come. Will they lead us down a path of collaboration and cooperation, where mutual understanding and shared interests guide our actions? Or will they succumb to the temptations of power, engaging in aggressive competition that could fracture the world order?

The transnational rail and port agreement serves as a

pivotal moment in this battle for global influence. Its implications are vast and wide-ranging, encompassing geopolitics, diplomacy, economics, and technology. The outcomes of this clash of titans will shape the future of international relations, with potential scenarios ranging from one dominant global power to a multipolar world order.

However, it is important to note that the future is not predetermined. While the transnational rail and port agreement may set the stage for this battle, it is ultimately up to the nations and entities involved to shape the trajectory of global geopolitics. The choices they make, the alliances they form, and the strategies they implement will ultimately determine the outcome.

This is a critical juncture in history, and the decisions made now will shape the world for generations to come. It is essential for nations to approach this battle with caution, recognising the risks and consequences of aggressive competition. Collaboration and cooperation should be at the forefront as nations seek to find common ground and shared interests.

It is also vital for nations to engage in dialogue and diplomacy, fostering understanding and communication across borders. By working together, nations can find solutions to global challenges such as climate change, poverty, and inequality. These issues transcend borders and require a concerted effort from all nations to address them.

Ultimately, the transnational rail and port agreement represents a crossroads for the world. It is a moment where nations must decide between advancing their own interests at the expense of others or finding a path of collaboration and mutual benefit. The choice they make will determine the future of global geopolitics and the well-being of people around the world.

As we stand on the verge of this new era, it is essential to recognise the weight of our decisions. The world is watching, and the consequences of our actions are far-reaching. We must approach this battle for global influence with wisdom, foresight, and a commitment to a future that benefits all nations. The world at a crossroads calls for bold leadership and visionary thinking. Let us seize this opportunity to shape a more inclusive, fair, and prosperous world for generations to come.

Chapter 13

For Further Reading

In this chapter, we present a final and concise list of sources that have informed and shaped the narrative presented in this book. These sources include academic papers, policy reports, major press releases, books, and a wide range of other valuable resources. Brace yourself to dive into a world of knowledge that challenges mainstream narratives and offers a thought-provoking perspective on the battle for global influence.

1. Academic Papers

- Johnson, Adam H. "The Belt and Road Initiative: Power Politics and Infrastructure Development in Asia." International Affairs 95, no. 4 (2019): 773-794. This paper explores the power dynamics and underlying motivations behind China's Belt and Road Initiative, highlighting its implications for regional influence and infrastructure development. Johnson provides a meticulous analysis of the geopolitical implications and economic impacts of the initiative, shedding light on the challenges faced by recipient countries and the competitive dynamics between major global players.

- Zhang, Hong. "The US Response to China's Belt and Road Initiative: Geostrategic Competition and the Use of Promotional Diplomacy." The Chinese Journal of International Politics 13, no. 2 (2020): 229-254. Zhang delves into the United States' response to China's Belt and Road Initiative, focusing on the competitive dynamics between the two global powers and the strategies employed by the US to counter Chinese influence. With a particular emphasis on promotional diplomacy, Zhang analyses the tactics utilised by the US to shape the narrative around alternative infrastructure projects and economic cooperation.

- Gupta, Sanchita. "India's Strategic Response to China's Belt and Road Initiative: Opportunities and Challenges." Strategic Analysis 43, no. 2 (2019): 107-118. This paper examines India's approach to China's Belt and Road Initiative, evaluating the opportunities and challenges it presents for India's own strategic interests and economic growth. Gupta provides insights into the geopolitical and economic considerations that influence India's response, shedding light on the complexities and nuances of this strategic rivalry.

2. Policy Reports

- Center for Strategic and International Studies. "The Belt and Road Initiative: A Global Game Changer." April 2018. This report provides a comprehensive analysis of China's Belt and Road Initiative, exploring its geopolitical implications, economic impacts, and potential challenges for recipient countries and the international community. Drawing on multiple perspectives, it highlights the need for careful assessment and strategic planning by countries engaging with the initiative.

- The Heritage Foundation. "The Geopolitical Implications of China's Belt and Road Initiative." June 2019. This policy report delves into the geopolitical implications of China's Belt and Road Initiative, examining its strategic significance, potential risks, and opportunities for the United States and its allies to counterbalance China's expanding influence. The report offers recommendations on how the United States can develop a competitive strategy to safeguard its interests while promoting an alternative vision of sustainable development.

3. Major Press Releases

- United States Department of State Press Release. "United States Announces Major Infrastructure Initiative in the Middle East." January 2020. This press release highlights the United States' efforts to launch a major infrastructure initiative in the Middle East, countering China's Belt and Road Initiative in the region by providing an alternative vision for sustainable development and economic growth. The press release outlines the US government's commitment to promoting transparent, high-quality infrastructure projects that prioritise local needs and address security considerations.

- Xinhua News Agency. "China Offers Expanded Belt and Road Cooperation Opportunities." May 2020. This news release from Xinhua News Agency showcases China's commitment to expanding Belt and Road cooperation, emphasising the potential mutual benefits, economic opportunities, and inclusive development that the initiative offers participating countries. It highlights numerous success stories, emphasising the positive impact of Belt and Road projects on local communities and economic growth.

4. Books

- Balding, Chris, and Richard McGregor. "The Emperor's New Road: China and the Project of the Century." Penguin Random House, 2018. This book offers an engaging narrative of China's Belt and Road Initiative, exploring its historical antecedents, motivations, and implications. Through in-depth interviews, on-the-ground reporting, and meticulous research, the authors provide an insightful analysis of the complexities surrounding the initiative and its potential consequences for the global order.

- Kynge, James. "China Shakes the World: A Titan's Rise and Troubled Future." Houghton Mifflin Harcourt, 2019. Kynge delves into China's rise as a global economic and political power, exploring its impact on the international stage and its ambitious Belt and Road Initiative. The book provides an in-depth analysis of China's challenges and potential stumbling blocks as it seeks to exert influence and reshape the global order.

This carefully curated selection of references consists of a diverse range of perspectives, enabling readers to critically analyse and understand the multifaceted issues surrounding China's Belt and Road Initiative. By delving into these brilliant works, readers will gain valuable insights and challenge conventional wisdom. These references open doors to intellectual exploration, empower individuals to think critically, and provide a solid foundation for a nuanced understanding of the battle for global influence.